Contents

KU-133-017

1

the rules of the game

The apparent complexities of chess, and the phenomenal skills of the greatest players, can make the game intimidating to some, but a basic understanding of chess, and an ability to appreciate the ideas of even the world champions, ought to be within the reach of everyone. Whatever your chess ambitions, you will surely find that the greater your understanding of the game, the more you will enjoy it and appreciate its beauty.

By introducing the basic moves of the pieces, the special rules and the essential laws of chess, this chapter will provide you with the first steps on that journey of understanding. As a complete beginner you may struggle to remember the rules that lay down how each piece may move. Once that hurdle has been overcome, the next stage is to avoid blundering away one's pieces by putting them where they can be captured, and to detect the opponent's most basic threats. When the blunders have been mostly eliminated, playing the game becomes a true art.

The first diagram shows the chessmen set up for the beginning of a game of chess. One player sits behind the white men and conducts their operations; his opponent faces him across the board, deciding the moves for the black pieces.

Each of the different chess pieces has its own individual mode of moving. Much of the charm and beauty, and indeed much of the difficulty, of the game of chess lies in the manner of the cooperation and conflict between pieces with distinct patterns of movement.

Before proceeding with the pieces, we must begin with a brief word about the board itself. This consists of sixty-four squares, in an eight-by-eight array, the squares coloured alternately light and dark, referred to respectively as the white squares and black squares. The board is always set out with a white square at the right-hand corner of each player. The white pieces at the start of the game occupy the back rows. From left to right, along the back row, Rook, Knight, Bishop, Queen, King, Bishop, Knight, Rook, with the eight Pawns filling the row in front of them. The rear line of black pieces are the same as their white counterparts directly facing them.

Each Queen thus begins the game on a square of her own colour: White's Queen on the left of her King, Black's on the right of her King.

The players make their moves alternately, White beginning the game. A move involves the transference of a piece from one square to another. No player may make two consecutive moves, neither may a player 'pass' when it is his turn to move.

Most of the chess pieces move in straight lines and their powers are simply grasped. There are three important and obvious types of straight line on the board: the *files* running up and down the board; the *ranks* running side to side; and the *diagonals*, lines of squares of the same colour, running at 45° angles to the ranks and files.

The ranks and files provide a convenient coordinate system for describing the chess moves. Each square on the board lies on one of the eight ranks and one of the eight files. The ranks are numbered from 1 to 8 beginning at White's side of the board; the files are lettered from a to h, left to right as viewed by White. Thus each square may be uniquely identified by a letter-number pair.

Moves of the pieces

The Rook

The ranks and files are the domain of the Rook, which can move as far as desired across empty squares up, down or across the board in a straight line. On an empty board a Rook, whatever square it is on, thus has a choice of 14 squares to which it may move: seven on the vertical line of squares through its own square, seven on the horizontal line.

The Bishop

Bishops traverse the board along the diagonals, and may travel as far as they like along squares of the same colour. As with the Rook, the Bishop may only travel over empty spaces; if its path is impeded by the presence of another piece, it cannot 'jump over'. Each Bishop can never leave the squares of the colour on which it began the game.

The diagram below shows the moves of Rook and Bishop. Each may travel to any square shown on the path of the arrows through it. As can be seen, a Bishop in the middle of the board has the choice of up to 13 squares, whereas one in the corner only has seven possible moves.

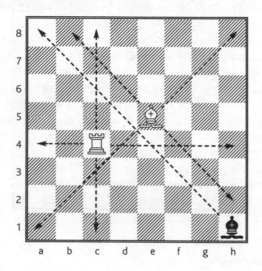

The Queen

The Queen is the most powerful piece on the board. She can move in straight lines along ranks, files or diagonals, so from any square she combines the possible moves of the Rook with those of the Bishop.

The King

The two Kings have a special role in the game, since the object of the game, as laid down in the rules, is the pursuit and capture of the enemy King. We shall come to that in a moment; for the time being, it is only necessary to know that the King has the shortest move of all – just one square in any direction.

The diagram below illustrates the moves of King and Queen. In the centre of the board the Queen commands 27 squares. The King never has more than eight.

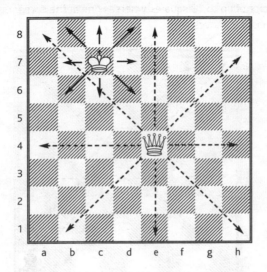

The Knight

There are many, perhaps too many, ways to describe the move of the Knight, the only chess piece which appears not to move in straight lines. His is a two-square move, bisecting the path of Rook and Bishop. In the diagram overleaf it is illustrated as one square like a Rook followed by a square in the manner of a Bishop, still moving away from the square of the original departure. Some prefer to think of the Knight's move as two squares vertically followed by one to the side, or two to the side and one up or down. However one chooses to describe it, the Knight's move is more easily visualized than explained. It should be mastered without difficulty, and with practice will come to be viewed as a single move from square to square, rather than a combination move involving change of direction.

The diagram below illustrates the eight possible Knight moves from a centre square. The white Knight may move to any of the squares indicated by the arrow-tips. Note that the Black Knight in the corner has its possible moves reduced to two.

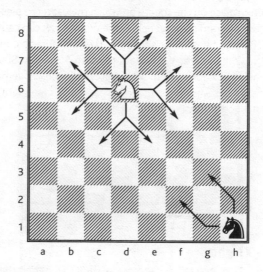

Unlike Rook, Bishop and Queen, the Knight cannot be impeded by other men in its path. The Knight gives the impression of being able to 'jump over' pieces, though one might equally well say that it can move between them. Whereas Rook, Bishop and Queen may be viewed as having lines of action along which they can move as far as desired, the Knight, like the King, has only a limited length of move. Rook, Bishop or Queen can reach any square on an empty board from any other in not more than two moves (provided the square is the appropriate colour in the case of the Bishop). A Knight can take as many as six moves to make a desired journey between two squares.

Capturing

Capturing enemy pieces

If an enemy man stands on a square to which a piece could otherwise move, that man may be captured. The capture is effected by removing the man to be captured from the board and placing the capturing piece on the square on which the captured piece stood. In the diagram position below, the White Rook can capture the Black Bishop, if it is White's move, or the Black Bishop could capture the White Knight, if it is Black to move. Note that Black's Bishop blocks the Rook's line of action, preventing its movement to the last two squares up the board, just as the White Knight hampers its progress sideways.

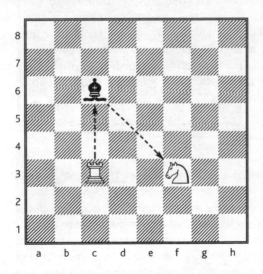

In chess, capturing is optional. If White chooses to capture the Bishop with his Rook, he simply removes the Bishop, replacing it with the Rook. Equally he may prefer to move the Rook or any other piece as he chooses, with or without a capture. The King is the only piece which may not be captured, for loss of the King signifies the end of the game. Attacks on the King will be discussed later. Whereas Rook, Knight, Bishop, Queen and King may in general capture anything along their lines of action (the King may make captures just as any other piece; the need to protect him from capture does not preclude his taking part in the carnage), the Pawn has special rules for its capturing moves. The Pawn is, in fact, exceptional in many ways, which we now explain.

The Pawn

The normal move of the Pawn is simple: it plods just one square forwards at a time. It alone of the chess pieces may never move backwards. On its *first* move, however, the Pawn may, if desired, be moved two squares forward instead of just one. That privilege is accorded to each of the eight Pawns on either side, but a Pawn may only advance two squares if both those squares are unoccupied, and the Pawn has not previously been moved.

As distinct from its forward mode of travel, the Pawn *captures* diagonally, but again only one square. It may not capture straight forwards.

White's legal Pawn moves in the previous diagram position are to any of the squares indicated by the arrows. The Black Bishop or Black Knight may be captured in the usual way, by removing the black piece from the board and replacing it with the capturing Pawn.

There are two further special rules involving Pawns. The first is their ability to promote. If a Pawn succeeds in making its way the full length of the board, arriving finally on the opponent's back line, then it may be promoted into any piece of the same colour other than a King. So if a White Pawn reaches the end of the board, it is removed and replaced by Queen, Rook, Knight or Bishop at the discretion of the White player. Promotion takes place immediately the Pawn reaches the end square; it cannot remain a Pawn. Usually the promoted Pawn is turned into a Queen, but as we shall see later there are circumstances where an apparently lesser piece may be preferable.

The final special rule for Pawns is the **en passant** capture, often improperly learned by beginners, but not really complicated. The diagram below shows a typical situation in which the en passant rule may apply.

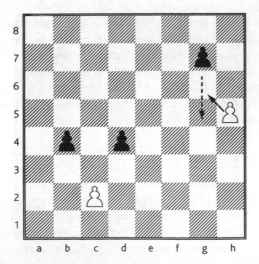

Any Pawn which advances two squares in a single move, passing over a square on which it could have been captured by an enemy Pawn, may still be captured by an enemy Pawn on that square just as if it had only advanced a single square. Thus, if the Black Pawn in the diagram position on the previous page advances two squares, it may be captured by White's Pawn as indicated by the arrow. Black's Pawn is removed from the board and White's is moved to the empty square over which it passed. Equally, if the other White Pawn were to advance two squares, it could be captured in exactly the same fashion by either of the neighbouring Black Pawns.

The privilege of capturing en passant is only extended for the single move following the two-square advance of an enemy Pawn. As with other captures, the en passant Pawn capture is optional (except, of course, in the rare case of no other legal move being available), but the option expires as soon as another move is played on the board. If an en passant capture is not made as soon as the opportunity is created, then the Pawn may never be captured en passant at all. Only Pawns may capture, or be captured, en passant. And the capture may only take place immediately after a two-square advance of the Pawn to be captured.

As we shall see later, the special abilities of the Pawn to promote, and to a lesser extent to capture en passant, play a significant role towards the end of well-contested games when the heavier pieces may have vanished from the board by exchanges and the emphasis shifts from direct attacks to the careful nurturing of the Pawns in their journeys in search of promotion.

We are almost at the end of this explanation of the moves of the pieces, but there is just one more exceptional move to consider.

Castling

As we have seen, a normal move consists of a player taking one of his own pieces and changing its square on the board, with or without the capture of an enemy piece. There is just one exception to this rule: a double move of King and Rook known as **castling**. The privilege of castling is a method to enable the King to escape from the centre of the board, and for the Rook to come closer to the middle. Castling may take place only between a King and a Rook both still unmoved on the squares upon which they began the game.

Castling is effected by moving the King two squares along the back rank towards the Rook, then placing the Rook on the square over which the King has passed. The diagram below indicates the situation of King and Rook after castling. Castling may take place with either Rook; in each case, the King moves two squares and the Rook apparently 'jumps over' the King. In the diagram, White has castled with his Rook on the King's side of the board, Black with the Rook on his Queen's side. (The two halves of the board are often referred to as 'King's side' and 'Queen's side' or K-side and Q-side for short. Castling in each direction is often termed *castling long* – on the Q-side – or *castling short* – on the K-side.)

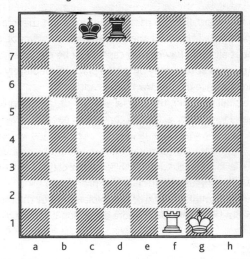

Castling may only be executed if the following conditions apply:
1 Neither the King nor the Rook taking part in the castling procedure has yet moved in the game.
2 The square upon which the King stands, the one over which it will pass, and the square upon which it will land must none of them be under attack from a hostile piece.

Note that this second condition only refers to the King; it does not matter if the Rook is under attack or, in the case of Q-side castling, if it passes over an attacked square. Thus in the position below, White may castle, since his King does not pass over any threatened square (though his Rook does). Black may not castle on either side: on the short side, his King would land on an attacked square; on the long side, his King would have to pass over an attacked square.

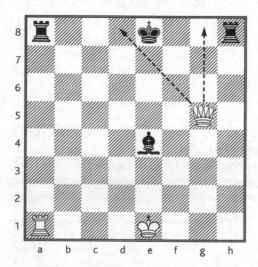

In practice, castling is best executed by moving the King first, then the Rook. If the King moves first, there can be no ambiguity of intention and no suggestion that only the Rook move was intended. (Theoretically, of course, castling is a simultaneous movement of Rook and King, but most chess players refrain from demonstrations of ambidexterity.)

These rules for castling may seem strange, but they are a consequence of the special importance of the King in the game of chess. The unique position of the King, that he must at all costs be preserved and protected from attacks, is one of the main features which distinguish chess from other board games in which the object may be simply to eliminate all the opponent's men. In chess, the ultimate objective is solely to capture the enemy King. Capture of his other pieces may only be a means to facilitate the final chase and submission of His Majesty.

Check and checkmate

When the King is threatened with capture by a hostile piece, it is said to be **in check** from that piece. Since the King must be preserved from capture, the rules specify that the player whose King is in check must immediately play a move to nullify the attack on his King. (The announcement of 'check' used to be mandatory under the rules of the game; this is no longer the case.) The diagram position below shows the White King in check from the Black Rook. The arrowed moves indicate White's possible replies and illustrate the three possible ways of responding to a check:

1 The King may move to a square on which he is no longer under attack;
2 The checking piece may be captured;
3 A piece may be interposed between King and checking piece to interrupt the line of action so that the King is no longer in check.

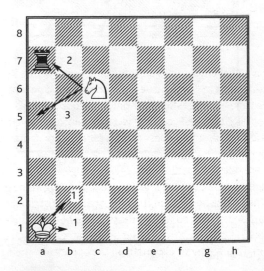

One of these modes of escaping from check must be employed. There is no question of leaving one's King in check in the hope that the opponent will not notice. That is simply against the rules.

Neither is it permissible to counter-attack by ignoring one's own King's safety and threatening the opponent's King. The first King to fall loses the game, so retaliatory regicide is not permitted.

If there is no legal move available which allows a checked King to escape – no piece can interpose or capture the checking piece, and the King cannot move anywhere out of attack – then the King is said to be in **checkmate** and the game is over, lost by the side whose King is checkmated. The diagram below gives an example of checkmate. Black's King is in check from the Rook; it cannot advance to escape from the check, because those squares are controlled by the White King or the White Knight.

At first sight it may seem that the White Rook can be captured by the Black Knight, but that is impossible since it would leave Black's King in check from the Bishop. So the game is over, and White is the winner. More examples of checkmate will be found in the exercises at the end of this chapter.

Stalemate

Finally, what happens if a player is not in check, but he has no legal move which does not leave his King in check? In that case we have reached what is called **stalemate** and the game is a draw. In normal parlance, stalemate is used to signify almost any state of dynamic equilibrium, particularly in political or military situations where each side in a conflict cannot make progress for fear of a devastating response from the other. In chess, however, stalemate has only this single technical usage: a position in which the side to move is not in check, but has no legal move available. Under the laws of the game, the result is then declared a draw. The diagram below illustrates a possible stalemate. Black to play is not in check, but none of his pieces can make a legal move without exposing the King to check.

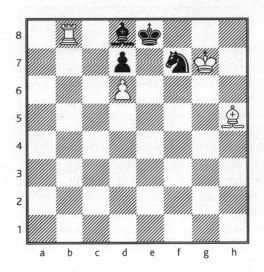

Though only a comparatively rare occurrence, stalemate has an important role to play in the defence of some difficult endgame positions where only a few pieces remain on the board. Many are the unfortunate beginners, too, who have blundered into stalemating their opponents' lone Kings when expectantly closing in for the kill with vast superiority in forces.

So far, we have seen two ways of ending the game: checkmate and stalemate. In practice, a game of chess does not usually go this far. Especially at a high level of play, when one side realizes that he is hopelessly behind, and knows that his opponent has the skills to pursue his advantage to victory, he does not carry on the struggle to the bitter end, with his King checkmated. Rather offer a timely resignation and begin another game in the hope of better fortune.

Just as a game may be won by checkmate or the opponent's resignation, there is more than one way for a game to be drawn. We have already met the draw by stalemate. Our final addition to the rules of chess is to explain other manners of draw.

Draws other than stalemate

1 **Draw by agreement** Just as a player may resign when he realizes his cause is hopeless, the two players may agree to call the game a draw if they agree that neither is getting anywhere and to continue would be pointlessly boring. In such circumstances, one player may 'offer a draw', which his opponent may accept or decline. In the case of acceptance, the game is over and the honour shared; in the case of a draw offer being declined, play simply proceeds as though nothing has happened.

2 **Draw by repetition** This is the rule which permits termination of a game if the pieces are just moving backwards and forwards. Specifically, if the same position has occurred three times on the board, with the same player to move in each case, then a draw may be claimed. In practice this almost always occurs when both sides are moving a single piece each, backwards and forwards, but the rule does

apply also to circuitous routes of reaching identical positions. All that matters is that the positions of all the pieces on the board are identical at three distinct moments in the game, and that it is the same player's turn to move on each occasion. (In fact the rule was recently further refined to specify also that the same possibilities, such as castling and en passant, are available in the position on each occasion, but such subtleties need not concern us at this stage.)

3 The Fifty-move Rule This is another device to prevent the game meandering on pointlessly. If 50 moves have been made by each side, without either moving a Pawn or making a capture, then the game may be declared drawn if either side wishes.

Neither of these last two rules need really concern the beginner, but we mention them here for the sake of completeness.

Those then are the basic rules of chess. Each piece with its own distinct move, cooperating with the others to try to checkmate the enemy King. How to set about that task will be the theme of the remainder of this book. Our last duty now is to become familiar with chess notation.

Notation

Unfortunately there are two different modes of chess notation currently prevalent in English-speaking countries. The old 'Descriptive Notation' has almost faded away, after a long fight, giving way to the simpler 'Algebraic Notation'. The latter will be used throughout this book. Since many old chess books in English are written in the other notation, there are advantages to becoming bilingual, but for the purposes of this introduction to the game, let us stick with the Algebraic system of chess notation.

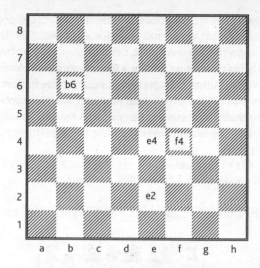

Firstly, the squares of the chessboard: as mentioned earlier, the files are lettered a–h from left to right as White views the board. The ranks are numbered 1–8 from near to far from White's side. Each square thus acquires a unique coordinate corresponding to its file and rank. The sixth square on the b-file is known as b6. The fourth square on the f-file is f4 and so on. If White moves the Pawn in front of his King two squares forward at the start of a game, that Pawn advances from e2 to e4. The pieces themselves are identified by their initial letters: K (King), Q (Queen), B (Bishop), R (Rook) and (with a little poetic licence, to avoid confusion with King) N for Knight. The humble Pawn is left without any identifying symbol.

In order to record any move on the chessboard, it is usually sufficient to write the symbol of the piece moved, together with the coordinates of the square to which it moves. Thus Nf3 means that a Knight has moved to square 3 on the f-file. Ra5 signifies a Rook move to the fifth square on the a-file. Remember that the numbering is always from *White's* side of the board.

The Black King and Queen always begin the game on e8 and d8 respectively. In the case of a Pawn move, we just write the square to which the Pawn moves, the absence of any piece symbol being taken as a sign that a Pawn has moved. Moves are numbered (either from the very start of a game or from the start of play from an indicated position), a single number including the White move and Black reply. A few moves will indicate how the system works. From the initial position, play may begin:

1 e3 Nc6 2 c4 a5 3 Nc3 Nb4

You should have reached the following position:

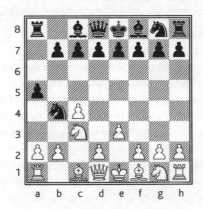

Now suppose White wishes to move his Knight from g1 to e2. It is not sufficient to write Ne2, because either White Knight can be moved to that square. In this case we specify Nge2 (meaning the Knight on the g-file goes to e2) or we could write N1e2 (the Knight on the first rank moves to e2). In either case the additional symbol, between the piece-letter and the square-coordinates, distinguishes between two similar pieces which can play to the same square.

So let us continue this imaginary game:

4 Nge2 Nd3, reaching the diagram position shown below and it is all over. The White King is in check from the Knight.

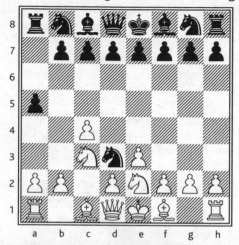

The King cannot move (you cannot capture your own pieces) and the checking piece cannot be taken. There is no question of interposing any piece along the checking line, because the Knight's mode of travel does not allow any such interruption. White is checkmated and the game is over.

That interlude was our first complete game, but it interrupted the explanation of chess notation. Just a few further points: captures are signified by the symbol '**x**' between piece and square. So Nxb5 means that a Knight makes a capture on square b5. The captured piece is not identified. In the case of a Pawn capture, we identify the capturing Pawn by the letter corresponding to its file. So bxc5 means that a Pawn from the b-file has made a capture on square c5. The symbol '+' is used to signify a move which delivers check. For checkmate, we write simply 'mate'. And last of all, castling is written as 0-0 or 0-0-0 for K-side or Q-side castling respectively.

For ease of reference, there follows a summary of the rules of chess and the manner of notation which will be followed throughout this book.

Exercises

1 The Knight's move sometimes presents a problem in familiarization; the following problems may be used to provide practice.
   (a) What is the shortest number of moves needed for a Knight to travel from one square to an adjacent square of opposite colour?
   (b) How many moves to reach a diagonally adjacent square?
   (c) How many moves to reach h8 starting at a1?

2 Which side can give immediate checkmate, if it is his turn to move in this position?

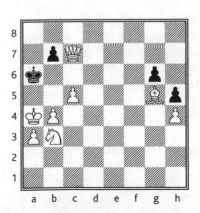

3 Black to play here checks the White King with 1 ... b5+ (the three dots before the move indicate that it is a Black move). Is this checkmate? What happens now?
See Chapter 5 for answers.

2

elementary endgames

Although it may seem paradoxical that we start our discussion of chess with the endgame, there is no better way to familiarize oneself with the powers of the pieces than to study positions when only a few men remain on the board. Their paths are unhampered by other pieces and the uncluttered board allows them full scope. In this chapter, we shall look at the procedures needed to win the game, if indeed it can be won, when the opponent has been reduced to a lone king. As will be seen, the principle is almost always the same: restrict the enemy King to a portion of the board by erecting a barrier with one's own men through which he cannot pass. The King's range is then gradually decreased until he is forced to the edge of the board where he is finally checkmated. The final section of this chapter will be devoted to positions with King and Pawn against King. The play in such an endgame can be very delicate and subtle.

Checkmate with two Rooks

This endgame gives a simple and dynamic demonstration of the power of Rooks and also the clearest display of a forcing back procedure. The White King plays no part. From the diagram position below, play continues **1 Rh4 Kf5 2 Ra5+** (one Rook controls the fourth rank, preventing the Black King from advancing, the other gives check, to force him further back) **2 ... Kg6 3 Rb4 Kf6 4 Rb6+ Ke7 5 Ra7+ Kd8 6 Rb8 mate**.

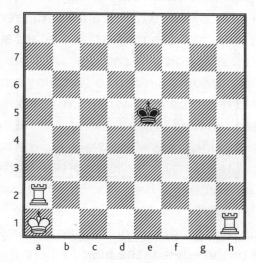

The procedure was sufficiently simple to repeat the same trick, each time one rank further down the board. The side with the two Rooks may, of course, choose instead to force the King to his doom on the first rank instead of the eighth, or to meet his end on the a- or h-file. One edge of the board is much the same as any other once the Pawns have disappeared from the scene of battle.

Now we shall see that in fact one of those Rooks was strictly superfluous to requirements, since King and Rook alone is sufficient to win, but here the White King plays an essential part in the procedure.

Checkmate with one Rook

Begin in the position of the previous diagram, but with the Rook on a2 removed from the board. Play may continue *1 Kb2 Kd5 2 Kc3 Ke5 3 Kd3 Kd5 4 Rh5+*.

This is the standard formation designed to force the Black King to give ground. The Rook checks while the White King stands guard to prevent the advance of Black's monarch.

To continue: *4 ... Kd6 5 Ke4 Kc6 6 Kd4 Kb6 7 Kc4 Kc6 8 Rh6+* (reaching the same formation, one rank further down the board) *8 ... Kd7 9 Kd5 Ke7 10 Ra6* (waiting) *Kf7 11 Ke5 Kg7 12 Kf5 Kf7* (or *12 ... Kh7 13 Rg6 Kh8 14 Kf6 Kh7 15 Kf7 Kh8 16 Rh6 mate*) *13 Ra7+ Ke8 14 Ke6 Kd8 15 Rh7* (waiting) *Kc8 16 Kd6 Kb8 17 Kc6 Ka8 18 Kb6 Kb8 19 Rh8 mate*.

Note, incidentally, that *19 Rb7* on the final move would be an example of stalemate. In chess notation the signs ! and ? are used to indicate good and bad moves, respectively. We would certainly adorn *19 Rb7* with ?? – a very bad move indeed.

King and Rook can in fact force mate against King in at most 13 moves from any position. The optimal strategy involves a readiness to switch one's objective from a mate on the back rank, as illustrated above, to a mate on the a- or h-file according to the direction the enemy King runs.

Other mates against a lone King

King and Queen against King

Strictly speaking this section ought to be unnecessary, since King and Queen can mate in exactly the same manner as King and Rook. The Queen's extra powers, however, do add some further points worth mentioning.

In the diagram position below, White has two moves which give immediate checkmate: *1* Qd8 or *1* Qb7.

Neither of these moves would be checkmate with a Rook. Note also that *1* Qc6?? would deliver stalemate and a draw. Another stalemate position would be with the Black King on a8, White Queen on b6 or c7 and White's King anywhere at all.

The Queen is just powerful enough to stalemate on her own, but she needs the aid of the King to deliver checkmate.

The mating positions with Rook or Queen against King should be understood and remembered. They translate with surprising ease into apparently complex middlegame positions.

King and two Bishops against King

One may easily convince oneself that there is no mating position with King and Bishop against King (although stalemate is possible). King and two Bishops, however, can force victory, provided, of course, the Bishops operate on opposite coloured squares. Remember, it is possible to have two white-squared Bishops or two black-squared Bishops following a Pawn promotion. Let us begin then with White's King and both Bishops on their home squares, e1, c1 and f1, and the Black King on e8. After the moves *1 Ke2 Ke7 2 Ke3 Ke6 3 Ke4 Kd6 4 Be3 Kc6 5 Bc4 Kd6 6 Bd4* we reach the diagram position.

Note how the Bishops on adjacent squares effectively control interlocking diagonals to restrict the Black King to a triangle of twelve squares from a8 to c6 and d6 to f8. The mating process consists in shrinking this triangle:

6 ... Kc6 7 Ke5 Kd7 8 Bd5 Kc7 9 Bc5 Kd7 10 Bd6 Kd8 11 Be6 Ke8. Now the King is confined to the back rank; the final stage is to force him into a corner where checkmate will be delivered:

12 Kf6 Kd8 13 Bb8 (waiting) *Ke8 14 Bc7 Kf8 15 Bd7 Kg8 16 Kg6 Kf8 17 Bd6+ Kg8 18 Be6+ Kh8 19 Be5 mate*. The final zig-zag process is particularly attractive.

King, Bishop and Knight against King

By far the most difficult of the 'elementary' mates, the Bishop and Knight mate necessitates forcing the enemy King not only to the edge, but right to the corner of the board. A forced mate is in fact only possible in the corner of the same colour as that of the squares upon which the Bishop travels. (Mate in the other corners is possible, but only if the defence errs.)

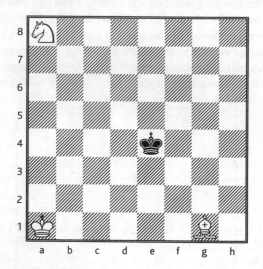

Begin in the diagram position, which is just about as bad as White could imagine in this endgame. The first stage must be to bring the white pieces closer together: *1 Kb2 Kd3 2 Nc7 Kc4 3 Ne6 Kd5 4 Nd4 Kc4 5 Kc2 Kd5 6 Kd3 Kc5 7 Bh2 Kd5 8 Nb3*. We have now reached a typical position in which Black must retreat. Note how White King,

Bishop and Knight cooperate to control squares round the Black King.
**8 ... Kc6 9 Kc4 Kb6 10 Nc5 Kc6 11 Na4! Kb7 12 Kb5 Kc8 13 Kc6
Kd8 14 Kd6 Kc8** (or *14 ... Ke8 15 Ke6 Kf8 16 Be5!* and the Black King
does not escape) **15 Nb6+ Kb7 16 Kc5 Ka6 17 Kc6 Ka5 18 Bd6 Ka6**.
Finally the King must be driven away from a8 towards a1 where the
Bishop will deliver mate. **19 Bb8! Ka5 20 Nd5! Ka4** (making a run
for it; instead *20 ... Ka6* demands less accuracy from White after
21 Nb4+ Ka5 22 Kc5 Ka4 23 Kc4 Ka5 24 Bc7+ continuing the
inexorable process towards a1) **21 Kc5 Kb3 22 Nb4! Kc3 23 Bf4! Kb3
24 Be5 Ka4 25 Kc4 Ka5 26 Bc7+ Ka4 27 Nd3 Ka3 28 Bb6** (waiting)
**Ka4 29 Nb2+ Ka3 30 Kc3 Ka2 31 Kc2 Ka3 32 Bc5+ Ka2 33 Nd3
Ka1 34 Bd6 Ka2 35 Nc1+ Ka1 36 Be5 mate**.

The most difficult part of the whole procedure is the
manoeuvre between moves 20 and 24, where Black's King appears
to be set free, only to find himself once again imprisoned by White's
pieces. The whole technique is an instructive example of using
one's pieces cooperatively, while it also illustrates well what a
cumbersome piece the Knight can be when it is trying to change
its object of attack at close range.

In all these examples of checkmates against a lone King, the
attacker occasionally made use of a waiting move. In chess, the
compulsion to move can sometimes be a disadvantage. When
there are many pieces on the board, a move can usually be found
which improves one's position, but in the endgame often only a
retreat is available when one would prefer to stand one's ground.
Indeed, if the privilege of 'passing' were allowed, none of the mates
with Rook, two Bishops, or Bishop and Knight, would be able to be
forced at all. This explains partly why so few of White's moves in
the Bishop and Knight mate are checking moves. White's pieces are
used to control squares round the Black King; there is no need to
attack the King directly since he must move anyway. Indeed White
cannot spare the resources to control the King's square as well as its
important retreats. Beginners are often tempted by the chance of a
check, but in such endgames there are usually better tasks for one's
pieces. As an exercise, you might like to attempt the King and Rook
mate, without giving any check before the final checkmate. As will

be seen, the process of gradual restriction is in fact more efficient than the forcing back by checking process given earlier.

Some comments on the endgame of King and two Knights against King will be found at the end of this chapter. Such technical endgames as these are rarely encountered in practical play, but the endgame we now discuss is of vital importance as perhaps the most commonly encountered finish to a closely contested game.

King and Pawn against King

The essential position to understand in this endgame is shown in the diagram below. Whichever side is to move, the game should end in a draw, but Black must play accurately to avoid letting the Pawn through to become a Queen.

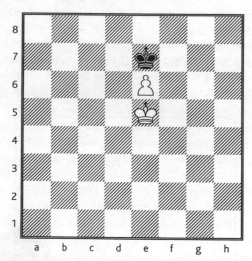

With Black to play the only good move is *1 ... Ke8!* There may follow *2 Kd6 Kd8 3 e7+ Ke8* and now *4 Ke6* is stalemate, while other moves lose the Pawn. Equally, after *1 ... Ke8! 2 Kf6 Kf8 3 e7+ Ke8 4 Ke6* is again stalemate.

Suppose instead Black had defended inaccurately with *1 ... Kd8?* Then after *2 Kd6 Ke8 3 e7* we have the same position but with Black, not White to move. He must give ground with *3 ... Kf7* when *4 Kd7* followed by *5 e8=Q* will win for White. The same happens, of course, after *1 ... Kf8 2 Kf6 Ke8 3 e7 Kd7 4 Kf7*, etc.

With White to move in the diagram position, he can do nothing to improve matters: *1 Kd5 Ke8! 2 Kd6 Kd8* or *1 Kf5 Ke8! 2 Kf6 Kf8* reach positions we have already examined. The important point is that Black must be able to answer Kd6, whenever it happens with Kd8 and Kf6 must be met by Kf8 to ensure that the critical position, with the Pawn one square from queening, is reached with the right player to move.

From this example, it follows that once the defender has occupied the square in front of the Pawn, he has little to worry about. For example, set up the position: White King on e3, Pawn on e4, Black King on e5. Play may continue *1 Kd3 Ke6 2 Kd4 Kd6 3 e5+ Ke6 4 Ke4 Kd7* (the purist will always play *4 ... Ke7*, but even the text move is good enough) *5 Kd5 Ke7 6 e6 Ke8!* and the draw is safe. Black has considerable freedom in his choice of earlier King moves, but when the Pawn reaches the sixth rank, he must take care.

If White's King is in front of his Pawn, however, it may be a totally different story.

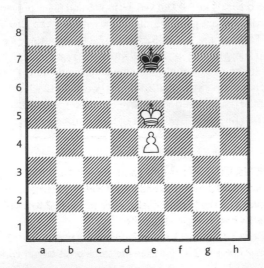

In this position, Black to move loses:

1 ... Kd7 2 Kf6! Ke8 3 Ke6 Kf8 4 Kd7 followed by the Pawn's direct march to the queening square. White's King prepares its path by outflanking the enemy King. Equally after **1 ... Kf7 2 Kd6 Kf6** (2 ... Ke8 3 Ke6 or 2 ... Kf8 3 Kd7) **3 e5+ Kf7 4 Kd7** and again the road is prepared for Pawn's advance. If, however, it is White's move in the diagram position, then he can only draw against best play: *1 Kf5 Kf7!* or *1 Kd5 Kd7!* and Black cannot be outflanked. After *1 Kf5 Kf7! 2 e5 Ke7 3 e6 Ke8!* we are back in familiar territory, safe for Black.

Now let us move all the pieces one square up the board: White's King on e6, Pawn on e5; Black King on e8. In this case, White wins whoever has the move. With Black to play: *1 ... Kd8 2 Kf7* or *1 ... Kf8 2 Kd7* ensures the triumph of the Pawn. With White to play, Black is still unable to reach the desired drawn position: *1 Kd6 Kd8 2 e6 Ke8 3 e7* and it is Black's move; he must give ground with *3 ... Kf7* when *4 Kd7* wins as usual.

Finally, let us move the pieces all one square back from their diagram positions: White King on e4, Pawn on e3; Black King on e6. Again with White to move, he can do no better than draw: *1 Kf4 Kf6* or *1 Kd4 Kd6 2 Ke4 Ke6 3 Kf4 Kf6* and Black prevents the White King from gaining ground. But with Black to play, White can win. For example, *1 ... Kd6 2 Kf5! Ke7 3 Ke5! (but not 3 e4 Kf7! 4 Ke5 Ke7! drawing) 3 ... Kf7 4 Kd6 Kf6 5 e4 Kf7 6 e5 Ke8 7 Ke6! Kd8 8 Kf7!*, etc. Always the White King prepares the Pawn's path before it advances, making sure that Black cannot reach the safety of the drawn position we have encountered earlier. As long as the White King can stay in front of his Pawn, he has chances for victory.

These conclusions are largely generalizable for any Pawn except for those on the a-file or h-file. We shall come to those in a moment. First, there is one tricky piece of play worth examining in the case of a Pawn one file in from the edge.

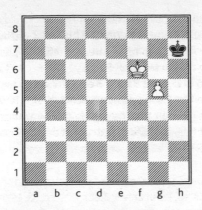

White wins with:

1 Kf7! Kh8 2 Kg6 Kg8 3 Kh6 Kh8 4 g6 Kg8 5 g7 Kf7 6 Kh7, etc.

White must not, however, play *1 g6+?*, when *1 ... Kh8! 2 Kf7* gives stalemate or *1 g6+? Kh8! 2 g7+ Kg8* leads to a familiar drawn position.

That example with a g-Pawn showed how the edge of the board can affect the result of a position. The stalemate possibility occurs only because there is no room to the right of the h-file. That has an even greater effect with a Pawn on the very edge file.

White seems to have all the advantages he could desire in this position, but he can only draw: **1 Kb6 Kb8 2 a6 Ka8 3 a7** stalemates the Black King, while instead **1 a6 Kc7 2 Ka8 Kc8 3 a7 Kc7** leaves White stalemated.

That completes our introduction to the basic checkmates against a lone King and the simple theory of King and Pawn against King. Many more complex positions can reduce to these elementary cases, so it is important to be familiar with them.

Further examples and exercises

1 If Black plays accurately White can only draw this position.
   1 Nf6+ Kh8? 2 Nf7 is mate, but after **1 ... Kf8!** instead, White can make no progress. Black can only lose such a position by blundering into a one-move mate.

Curiously, if we add a Black Pawn on e6, White can indeed win: **1 Ng4 e5 2 Nh6+ Kh8 3 Nf6 e4 4 Nf7** mate. Without the e-Pawn, Black would be stalemated after White's third move. In fact, there are many positions where two Knights can win against King and Pawn, but the procedure is generally long and complex.

2 This position of King and two Pawns against King looks as though White should win comfortably, but *1* Kh6? or *1* Kf6 give stalemate. In fact any attempt by the White King to approach closer suffers from the same result. The only way to win involves jettisoning one of the Pawns:

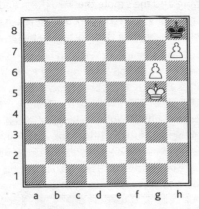

1 Kf5 Kg7 *2* h8=Q+! Kxh8 *3* Kf6 Kg8 *4* g7 Kh7 *5* Kf7 and wins.

Both these examples show that the mere existence of a piece on one's own side can actually be a disadvantage. In the second case, White could solve the problem by throwing it overboard.

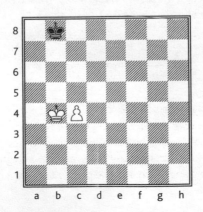

Finally, the lower diagram on the previous page shows a more complex example of King and Pawn against King. Black to play in this position; what should the result of the game be?

Try to work it out before reading the explanation below. The position should be drawn, but only if Black finds the correct first move: 1 ... Kc8!. The reason for this is as follows: After 1 ... Kc7? 2 Kc5! or 1 ... Kb7? 2 Kb5! we reach positions of a type already discussed and winning for White. (For example 1 ... Kc7 2 Kc5 Kb7 3 Kd6 Kc8 4 Kc6 Kb8 5 Kd7 and the Pawn is ready to romp home.) After 1 ... Kc8! Black keeps open his options and can meet 2 Kc5 with Kc7! or 2 Kb5 with Kb7! preventing the White King from gaining space in either case. Two Kings with just one empty square between them in such a manner (say on b5 and b7 or c5 and c7) are often said to be *in opposition*. The side who moved last has *taken the opposition* and is ready to follow his opponent (as Black does here to prevent White from gaining space) or to side-step and outflank him (as White does when Black is forced to step aside). The concept of the opposition is a particular example of the more useful one of *related squares*.

In our example above, White's Kb5 must be met by Kb7, and Kc5 must be met by Kc7; thus we have two pairs of related squares (b5, b7) and (c5, c7). On b4 White's King is in touch with both b5 and c5, so Black must stay in touch with b7 and c7. The only possibility therefore is 1 ... Kc8!.

elementary tactics

Chess players are often asked: 'How many moves do you see ahead?' The essence of chess thought lies in the ability to calculate correctly future possible continuation of the game, to see what is likely to happen several moves ahead and to select the most promising move on the basis of variations calculated. A key element of 'seeing ahead' comes from tactics (e.g. captures of pieces, checking moves and threats of checkmate). In this chapter we shall be considering the elements which make up tactical play in chess.

Relative values of the pieces

Rooks, Knights, Bishops, Queens and Pawns all have different ways of moving. A Queen can do all that a Rook can, and more. A Rook aided by its King can checkmate the enemy King on an empty board, whereas Bishop or Knight cannot. No surprise then to learn that a Queen is considered superior to a Rook, which in turn is generally worth more than a Bishop or Knight. One cannot assign absolute values to the pieces, since circumstances may drastically alter the effectiveness of each piece. As a rough and ready rule, the following scale of values gives an idea of the relative worth of each of the pieces:

Pawn – 1; Bishop – 3; Knight – 3; Rook – 5; Queen – 9.

One cannot assign a value to the King, since his special role in the game puts him beyond such material consideration. In terms of fighting ability, however, a King used as an attacking piece is approximately as effective as a Knight or Bishop. The need to keep him safe from attack, however, prevents the aggressive use of the King until all danger has vanished from the board. If we look at the nature of the other pieces, we can understand better how the above scale of piece values ought to be interpreted.

The Pawn

The humble foot-soldier of chess, weakest of all pieces, but in that very weakness lies the greatest strength of the Pawn. Any other piece must run from the Pawn's attack. If, for example, a Knight or Rook attacks a Pawn, it is sufficient to defend that Pawn with another man. Capturing the Pawn will then entail a net loss. On the other hand, if a Pawn attacks a Knight or Rook, the attacked piece can hardly stand its ground, even if defended by another piece, since its capture will entail loss of Knight or Rook for a mere Pawn.

The Pawns are thus the most effective pieces for controlling terrain on the chess battlefield. Knights, Bishops, Rooks and Queens dare not tread on those squares attacked by Pawns.

As we shall see when we come to discuss strategic planning, the Pawns define the boundaries of each side's territory. A planned and gradual advance of Pawns can gain manoeuvring space for the other pieces and cramp the opponent's men.

Bishops and Knights

Each worth about three Pawns, the Bishop and Knight are so different from one another that it is hard to understand how they can have so close a value. The Bishop is a long-range piece, quick to move from one area of the board to another, but limited always to squares of one colour. Thirty-two of the board's squares are permanently beyond its horizons. The Knight, on the other hand, can get anywhere, given the time.

Generally speaking, if the board is open and uncluttered by numerous Pawns, the Bishop is superior, particularly when there is action at widely separated points. The Bishop in such cases can affect both sides of the board at the same time; it can help with attack, while simultaneously looking backwards towards defence. When the Pawns have become blocked against one another, the diagonals are closed, and play is slow and localized, then the Knight is at its most effective.

While Knight and Bishop are of approximately equal value, the pair of Bishops are more often than not superior to two Knights. We have already seen that two Bishops can checkmate a lone King where two Knights cannot. The two Bishops, operating on different colour squares, complement each other perfectly. They can never impede each other's movements, and between them they can cover the whole board.

The Rook

In the early stages of the game, the Rook has a lesser part to play than its value might suggest. The Rook needs open lines: until some Pawns have been exchanged, the Rooks simply do not have the space they need to operate effectively. Also, since Rooks are fundamentally more valuable than Knights or Bishops, a Rook must run from attack by those lesser pieces. Any Rook brought out onto the open board too early is liable to find itself hounded about by attacks from sniping Bishops and Knights.

The table of values suggests that a Rook and one Pawn is worth about the same as Bishop and Knight, but such an exchange should be viewed with circumspection. Both Rooks and Pawns need time to make their value felt. As a Pawn advances, its eventual threat of becoming a Queen grows more real. As lines become open, the Rooks swing into action. But in the early stages of the game, Bishop and Knight in combination are likely to be more than a match for Rook and Pawn. Despite that, the calculation making Rook equal to Bishop and two Pawns, or Knight and two Pawns, is a fair approximation to the way things work in practice.

The Queen

Worth a little less than two Rooks, about the same as three lesser pieces (or minor pieces as Bishop and Knight are usually known). Interestingly, although the Queen moves like Rook or Bishop, she is worth more than the combined value of those two pieces. This reflects her ability to operate as a Bishop on white or black squares (though not, of course, simultaneously).

Forcing gain of material

The simplest way to gain material on the chessboard is to capture an undefended piece. When beginners start to play, and are still getting used to the moves of the pieces, most games are decided simply by overlooking that pieces are attacked, or by carelessly putting them on squares where they can be taken. Once one has overcome that phase of unfamiliarity with the pieces, such crude mistakes become rare. (I would like to say that they disappear, but sad experience tells that it is not so.) The next stage in the familiarization process is to understand the range of simple tactical tricks which can lead to gain of material in somewhat more sophisticated fashion. What follows in this chapter is a small-arms catalogue for the chessboard warrior.

There are really only two distinct ways of forcing gain of material: attacking two pieces at the same time, or attacking one

piece which, for one reason or another, cannot move away.
Each of these objectives may be achieved in a number of different ways, the most common of which will be illustrated in this chapter. All the ideas involved will be seen to be strongly dependent upon the geometry of the chessboard and the lines of action of the pieces.

In each of the examples which follow, you should try to improve your skills at visualizing the result of a series of moves. Set up the position on a board and play through the moves if necessary, but always return to the original position and attempt to replay the moves in your head, until you are capable of a clear visualization of the variation under consideration and the final position arrived at. This ability is bound to come gradually, and it is an essential part of chess fluency.

The first example of calculation, below, involves working out the result of a series of exchanges of pieces. Here it will be necessary to remember as the variation proceeds that pieces are disappearing from the board. There is no easy way to learn to keep track of such calculations, except by continual practice and increasing experience of the chessboard and pieces.

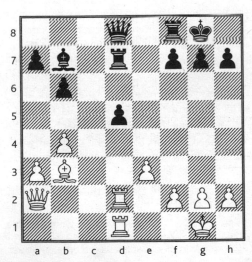

White to play calculates that he can safely capture the d-Pawn. Although only two of his pieces directly attack the Pawn, two more lurk with hidden attacks. Thus 1 Bxd5 Bxd5 2 Rxd5 Rxd5 3 Qxd5 Qxd5 4 Rxd5 and White has emerged with an extra Pawn. White's Queen and Bishop on the diagonal form in effect two attacks on the Pawn, as do his two Rooks on the file. Equally, Black's Queen provides a reserve defence. Reasoning that White has four effective attackers, while Black has only three defenders, is a tempting but fallacious argument that the Pawn can be taken. The order of capturing is of great importance as we can see if we place the White Queen on d3 instead of a2. White still has four attacks on the Pawn, but 1 Bxd5? Bxd5 2 Qxd5 Rxd5 3 Rxd5 does not compel Black to continue the capturing sequence; after 3 ... Qf6 White has just lost his Queen for Rook and Pawn. Of course a simple count of attackers and defenders can give a good guide to whether a particular capture is feasible or not, but there is no substitute for a precise calculation of all the moves involved.

The fork

The simplest tactical weapon to ensure gain of material is the **fork**: an attack on two different pieces by the same man. If the attacked pieces are both of higher value than the attacker, or if there is no satisfactory way to leave both pieces defended, then material loss may be inevitable. One of the shortest of all international chess games ended with a drastic fork: after the moves 1 e4 c5 2 d4 cxd4 3 Nf3 e5 4 Nxe5? Black played 4 ... Qa5+ when any move meeting the check will be met by 5 ... Qxe5 leaving Black a Knight ahead. The fork of King and Knight after Black's fourth move gives White no time to attend to both the attacks in a single move.

Unguarded pieces in the centre of the board are particularly susceptible to fall victim to a fork by the enemy Queen. Keeping all one's pieces protected all the time, even if it were possible, would be far too defensive an attitude, but special vigilance should be given to those of one's men which are not defended and are liable to attack by enemy pieces.

Since any piece may attack an enemy piece, it follows that any piece – even a King – may deliver a fork by attacking two enemy pieces simultaneously. The most commonly encountered, however, and the most easily overlooked is the Knight fork.

In the position of the next diagram, White can fork King and Rook with Nc7+ or King and Queen with Nf6+. In either case the King must move, leaving the other piece to be captured.

Many are the Rooks in the corner which have been lost, before they have even made a single move, to such a fork by a Knight.

The discovered attack

When a piece moves from one square to another, it will generally result in a change in the immediate effect of that piece. New squares will be attacked and defended, new threats created. After each move, one must naturally look at those changes to see what immediate action must be taken. But also the mere act of vacating a square can have important consequences. Lines of action previously blocked can suddenly become open for other pieces. When one piece steps aside to reveal an attack by another, we speak of a **discovered attack**.

In the position shown below, White, for all his material inferiority, can use the theme of discovered attack to win the game. After *1 Rxg7+ Kh8* the scene is set for a Rook move to discover a check from the Bishop: *2 Rxf7+ Kg8 3 Rg7+ Kh8 4 Rxd7+ Kg8*. By now the theme should be clear. White has a simply operating mechanism, allowing Black no option each time but to submit to the mercies of Rook and Bishop. *5 Rg7+ Kh8 6 Rxc7+ Kg8 7 Rg7+ Kh8 8 Rxb7+ Kg8 9 Rg7+ Kh8 10 Rxa7+ Kg8 11 Rg7+ Kh8 12 Rc7+ Kg8 13 Rxc8* and White is set for victory.

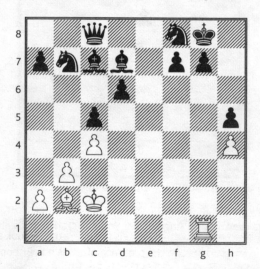

The discovered check is almost equivalent to a free move with the discovering piece. While the opponent is escaping from the check, that piece can do its worst. Of course, if the opponent's King is not at the end of the discovery, the effect is considerably lessened, but it can be as devastating for a vital attack to be discovered by a piece itself giving check.

In the next diagram, Black to play is set to discover an attack on the White Queen by moving his Knight. Playing **1 ... Nb4+** (or **1 ... Nd4+**) he ensures that the next move he will be able to play is **2 ... Rxg6**. Even if the Knight is captured, Black will gain Queen for Knight from the venture. Equally, if White is to play in the same position, he will move **1 Bd8+** followed by **2 Qxg4** gaining Queen for Bishop.

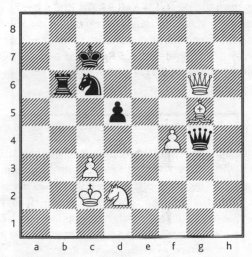

As with the fork, the theme of the discovered attack is that of attacking two enemy pieces at the same time. The lesson here is to look beyond one's own men which appear to be blocking their colleagues. The blockage may be purely temporary. The Black Knight on c6 only lessens rather than cancels the effort of the Rook along the rank from d6 to h6, and the presence of the White Bishop on g5 does not guarantee a safe life for the Black Queen on g4.

The pin

Even simpler than attacking two pieces at the same time is to attack one piece which cannot, or dare not, move away. The **pin** is one of the simplest ways to immobilize an enemy piece.

In this diagram position, White can immobilize the Black Knight by playing **1 Ba4**. The Knight cannot move away without leaving the Black King in check from the Bishop. The Bishop is said to *pin* the Knight to the King. After **1 ... Kd7**, Black defends his Knight, but the pin is not broken. Advancing his Pawn with **2 d5**, White ensures that he will win the Knight. It cannot move away and will be captured next move by Pawn or Bishop.

When a piece is pinned in such a manner to the King, the pin is absolute. The pinned piece cannot legally move away. But it can be almost equally immobilizing to have a piece pinned to the Queen or Rook. If we replace the Black King by a Queen in the position above, after *1 Ba4* the Knight is again pinned and cannot move without exposing the Queen to possible capture by the Bishop. In this case, however, there is a remedy in the shape of discovered attack: **1 ... Nxd4+!** followed by **2 ... Qxa4**, a tactical resource allowed by the position of the White King.

The essential feature of a pin is a piece immobilized by its duty of shielding a more important piece from attack. The following diagram illustrates a closely related tactic with the roles of the attacked pieces transposed.

White to play can win a Rook by **1 Ba3+**. Black's King must move out of attack, revealing an attack by the Bishop on the Rook. Equally, White could begin **1 Rh6+** and capture the Bishop on a6 after the King moves away.

If Black is to move in the diagram position he plays **1 ... Bb7+** to win the Rook on h1. Such attacks on one piece through another are sometimes called *X-ray attacks* or *skewers*. They combine geometrical features of both the pin and the discovered attack.

As one becomes familiar with these different types of tactic, one begins to develop an awareness for the presence of pieces on the same diagonal, rank or file. When, for example, Queen and King stand on the same file, it is natural to look for an enemy Rook which can move to that file to win the Queen by pin or X-ray. If King and Queen are on the same diagonal, one must be alert for a possible Bishop move onto that diagonal.

Simple tactics such as those described above are no more than one-move tricks to gain material advantage. In general, the complete tactical resources of a position will involve a complex interaction of these and other elementary units. When more than one piece, or more than one tactical idea, is involved in a forcing sequence of moves in a chess game, we have what is known as a **combination**. The diagram below gives a neat but simple example of a combination.

White begins with *1 e5+* (Pawn fork). If the Pawn is not captured, Black will lose his Queen. But *1 ... Kxe5* is met by *2 Bc3+* (X-ray attack on the Queen), or *1 ... Qxe5* by *2 Bg3* (pinning the Queen). On White's third move, come what may, he will be able to capture the Black Queen. Note how the initial Pawn advance in this short sequence forced the Black King and Queen onto the same diagonal, either a1–h8 or h2–b8, where the Bishop could then perform its duties. As White's most dynamic forcing move, *1 e5+* should be the first possibility one looks at in the position. Continuing with each of Black's available replies, the rest of the combination should be readily discovered. The difficulty of any combination often consists mainly in forcing oneself to give serious consideration to an introductory move (such as *1 e5+* above) which at first sight just leaves a man to be captured. In fact, one should give at least cursory examination to any move which severely restricts the opponent's choice of reply.

That example was only a diversion from the theme of elementary tactical ideas, to show how they can build into more complex structures. We have still to introduce two more of the bricks for such structures.

Undermining and overloading

When a piece has an important defensive duty to perform, that piece can be as tied to its post as if it were pinned. In the diagram position, the Black Knight on c6 guards the a7 Pawn and is the only obstacle to White's playing *1 Qxa7* mate.

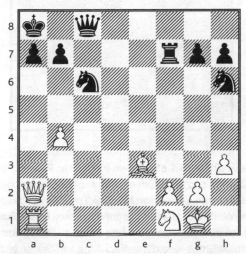

By attacking the Knight with *1 b5* White sets about undermining the defender of a7. *1 ... Na5* would be met simply by *2 Qxa5*, while other Knight moves all allow Qxa7 mate. So the Knight would have to be given up. An even simpler example of undermining a defender can be seen on the other side of the board. The Knight on h6 defends the Rook on f7. By playing *1 Bxh6* White gains a Knight since *1 ... gxh6* allows *2 Qxf7*. It is not enough to think complacently that all one's pieces are defended, it is necessary also that those defences cannot be undermined by capture or attack.

The idea behind a successful undermining operation is to eliminate the defender, but it can be equally effective to lure it elsewhere. A piece which tries to combine two important defensive duties can be unreliable when its workload demands that it be in two different places at the same time.

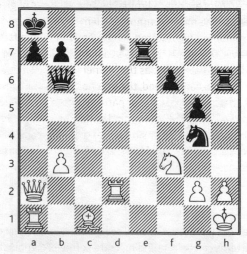

The diagram position gives examples of overloaded pieces. The Black Queen defends against both Rd8 mate and Qxa7 mate. White to move first lures away the defender then kills: *1 Rd8+ Qxd8 2 Qxa7 mate* (or *1 Qxa7+ Qxa7 2 Rd8 mate*). Turning our attention to the other side of the board, it is White's Knight which has too full an in-tray. Called upon to protect both h2 and e1, he cannot cope. Black to play wins with *1 ... Re1+ 2 Nxe1 Rxh2 mate*. (He could also start with *1 ... Rxh2+* but the mate would take a move longer.)

With the last couple of examples, we complete our introduction to the basic tactical themes, but we have already begun to tread on the ground of the next topic: basic mating patterns. The ultimate object of any chess game is checkmate. Winning the opponent's pieces will be a considerable help in attaining that objective, and we have already seen some of the ways of mating a lone King. But as these last positions have shown, a King can fall victim to checkmate even with many pieces on the board.

You may have noticed certain similarities between the mating positions reached in these examples and those in the previous chapter when the board was down to only a few men. This is no coincidence. There are only a limited number of ways of giving checkmate and the most common of them recur again and again with only minor features altered. As one becomes more familiar with the game, one builds up a repertoire of mating patterns, recognized immediately, just as the learner of a new language expands his vocabulary. Indeed, the psychologist would describe the skill of chess playing as one of pattern recognition. The position on the board is compared in the mind with positions one has previously encountered. Their similarities and differences are noted and old ideas are reassembled to create new combinations and new understanding.

Mating combinations

In the next few pages we shall see how the knowledge of simple mating patterns can help in finding quite complex combinations which may decide the outcome of the game. Much of chess thought might be described as visualizing a desired end position, then working out if such a position can be attained and how. The mating schema which follow give the ideas for the end positions. In the game positions following each mating pattern, the essential details of the pattern are all there, if not quite in the right places to deliver the fatal blow immediately. It is the job of the player to ascertain whether he can force the other bits of the jigsaw into place.

Needless to say, this collection is far from exhaustive. If it were, the game of chess would never have lasted as long as it has. What is important is to see how simple chessboard structures can transplant themselves into apparently more complex positions. Finding the winning continuation in such positions as these is a two-stage process: firstly, the inspirational stage of detecting the relevant idea;

and secondly the analytical process of establishing the sequence of moves which can turn the inspiration into reality on the board. Each part of this process is made easier or more difficult by the clues on the board that provide a guiding light towards solution.

The back-rank mate

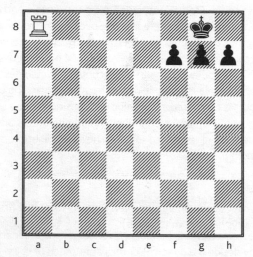

The theme of the back-rank mate is simple: a Rook or Queen gives check to a King which cannot escape owing to the presence of his own Pawns. Possible variations to the basic pattern include the substitution of a Black Bishop for the Pawn on h7; or a Knight could replace the f7-Pawn, with White's Rook closer in on e8. Leaving a King hemmed in on the back row in this manner is always a source of potential danger. This type of checkmate is one of the most common sudden finishes to games between inexperienced players. Of course, it is only a variation on the endgame mate with King and Rook against King; then it was the White King which replaced the three Black Pawns by standing guard at g6 to refuse any escape square to the Black monarch.

The simplest way to avoid the danger of a back-rank mate is to ensure that the King has an escape square by playing a Pawn to h6 or g6, but, like all chess moves, such a Pawn advance should only be made if there is real need for it.

In the examples below, we see one long and dazzling variation on this simple theme and one short but difficult game-ending which manages to rotate the idea through ninety degrees.

(i)

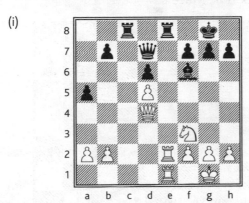

From a game Adams–Torre, New Orleans 1920 (the first-named player always has the white pieces):

1	Qg4!	Qb5
2	Qc4!	Qd7
3	Qc7!	Qb5
4	a4	Qxa4
5	Re4!	Qb5
6	Qxb7!	resigned.

Throughout this remarkable sequence of moves, Black's Queen and c8-Rook are tied to the defence of the Rook on e8. Any capture of White's Queen would be met by Rxe8+ followed by back-rank mate. After White's fifth move, the e4-Rook is immune (5 ... Rxe4 6 Qxc8+ Qe8 7 Qxe8+ Rxe8 8 Rxe8 mate). Finally the Black Queen has nowhere to hide and must be lost. Recognizing the hopelessness of playing on without his Queen Black conceded the game. (Recent research has cast doubt upon the authenticity of this game, but it is still a beautiful combination, real or invented.)

The next example features a neat defeat of a World Champion.

(ii)

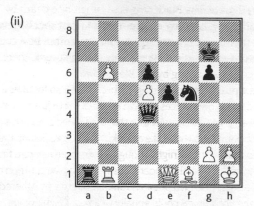

From the game Karpov–Taimanov, Leningrad 1977, the finish with Black to play was:

1 ... Ng3+! and White resigned.

2 Qxg3 Rxb1 leaves him no real chance, while 2 hxg3 Ra8! leaves no defence against 3 ... Rh8 mate. Not a back-rank but a side-edge mate.

Smothered mate

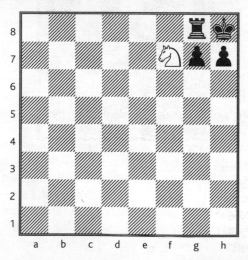

This mate by the Knight is usually known by the picturesque term **smothered mate**. The Black King is smothered to death by his own pieces denying him any escape from a Knight check. As we have seen, one's own pieces getting in the way can often be a cause of problems. Even in the basic Rook mate on the back-rank, there is an element of self-smothering by the Black Pawns.

The shortest possible game ending in checkmate also features a King surrounded by his own pieces. Known as **fool's mate** it is over in two moves: 1 f3 e5 2 g4 Qh4 mate. Note that the Queen does not even avail herself of the ability to move like a Rook, this is a pure Bishop mate.

Smothered mate with a Knight, though a comparatively rare finish to a game, is one of the best chessboard illustrations of the triumph of quality over quantity. Note two possible variations in this smothered mate position: the Rook on g8 could equally well be a Knight; or we could give mate with the Knight also on g6, provided we have a White Rook added on h1, pinning the Black h-Pawn to prevent capture of the Knight. The two examples below both illustrate a common combinational idea which leads to a victory by smothered mate.

(i)

White wins as follows:

1	Qc4+	Kh8
2	Nf7+	Kg8
3	Nh6+	Kh8
4	Qg8+!	Rxg8
5	Nf7	mate.

Note that Black's King cannot flee to f8 on the first or third moves of this sequence, owing to immediate mate by Qf7.

This combination is known as 'Philidor's Legacy' after the great French player (and operatic composer) François Andre Danican Philidor (1726–95). The idea, however, dates back still further to the Spaniard Luis de Lucena in 1497 and subsequently the Italian Gioachino Greco in 1625.

Three hundred years after Greco, the smothered mate was still effective in the game Stolberg–Zak, USSR 1938:

(ii)

1	Rd7!	Bxd7
2	Qxf7+	Kh8
3	Bc4!	Ng6
4	Qg8+!	Rxg8
5	Nf7	mate.

White's opening move disrupted communications between c7 and f7. His third move threatened Qg8 mate and also set up the mechanism for the smothered mate.

Mating with Queen

The simplest checkmate of all is given by a protected Queen sitting directly in front of a King on the edge of the board.

A Queen giving check in such a position will always end the game at once, provided she cannot be captured. A very common variation to this checkmate position is seen by placing the White Queen and Knight one square to the right. With that modification, the King has an escape square on f8, but the position becomes checkmate if f8 is occupied by a Black Rook, Bishop or Queen. The most frequently seen of all short beginners' games ends in just such a mate. Known as **scholar's mate** it runs: *1* e4 e5 *2* Bc4 Bc5 *3* Qh5 Nc6?? *4* Q**x**f7 mate. On his third move, Black saw the attack on e5 and defended the Pawn with his Knight, overlooking the far more deadly threat to f7. By playing either *3 ...* Qe7 or *3 ...* Qf6 both threats could satisfactorily have been defended and White's Queen later attacked and driven away from her threatening post.

Note that in all these Queen mate positions, it does not matter which piece defends the Queen: Knight, Bishop, Pawn or even King, the Queen herself covers all the possible flight squares of the enemy King, and the only function of the defender is to prohibit Black's capture of Queen with King.

The next position is from a game Betbeder–Tiroler, played in 1930. White's thoughts should be directed by the presence of his

Pawn so close to the Black King. If his Queen can join in the attack, the smell of checkmate should be in the air:

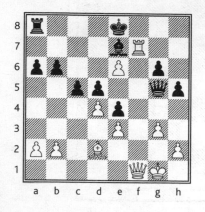

(i)

1	Rf8+!	Bxf8
2	Qf7+	Kd8
3	Qd7	mate.

The essence of this combination is the Rook's opening clearance of f7 for the Queen. Note that Black's forced capture of the Rook also opens the road for the final Queen move.

The chess player's thought process in such a position must, as always, be flexible. It is easy to think: 'I cannot play Rf8+, because he can take it', but forcing oneself to visualize the position after *1 ... Bxf8*, even momentarily, should reveal the easy mate which follows.

In that example, *1 Rf8+* was a forcing move which gave Black no time to organize his defences. The next position is a famous example of forcing play to reach a desired objective:

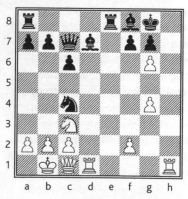

(ii)

1	Rh8+!	Kxh8
2	Rh1+	Kg8
3	Rh8+	Kxh8
4	Qh1+	Qh2
5	Qxh2+	Kg8
6	Qh7	mate.

(Mannheim v Regensberg, played in 1912.)

Mate with Rook and Knight

This mating position with Rook and Knight is a good illustration of the cooperation between two pieces of different types. The Knight both protects the Rook and covers the one possible square on which the Black King would not be in check from the Rook.

There is an interesting variation on this theme if we move the White Rook to d7 and the Black King to g8, in check from the Knight. Then 1 ... Kh8 will just walk into the above mating position by 2 Rh7, but the alternative King move 1 ... Kf8 can be met by 2 Nh7+ Ke8 3 Nf6+ Kf8 4 Nh7+ Kg8 5 Nf6+, etc. The Black King can never escape from the Knight checks and White would be able to claim a draw by repetition of position. Such a draw is termed a draw by **perpetual check**, when an endless series of checks forces the harassed King to repeat his moves. Several games have been saved by such a Rook and Knight perpetual check mechanism, with the checking side, of course, well behind on material, but having successfully manoeuvred his Rook and Knight into the right places to force the draw.

The next position is taken from an 1860 game won by the first World Champion, Wilhelm Steinitz. If White's Rook were not in the way Black could mate immediately with 1 ... Rg1. This observation should be enough to suggest the winning combination:

(i)

1	...	Qh4!
2	Rg2	Qxh2+!
3	Rxh2	Rg1 mate.

Throughout this short sequence, Black is simply taking advantage of the overloaded White Rook, which cannot combine its task of guarding g1 with the job of defending against a Queen and Knight mate.

The next example, from a game Sokolov–Ruzhnikov, USSR 1967, is a more imaginative use of the same idea. Black rejects the chance to promote his Pawn to a Queen, even with check, since White's reply would be to interpose the Rook, discovering check for his own Queen and winning Black's newly crowned lady. Instead his first move is an attempt to chase away the White Queen.

The end is short and drastic:

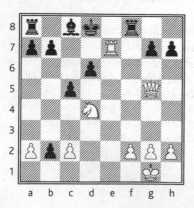

(ii)

1	...	h6
2	Rxb7+!	hxg5
3	Nc6+	Ke8
4	Re7	mate.

The usual Rook and Knight mate is translated into the middle of the board, with Black's own Rook plugging the last hole.

The last few pages have given some examples of how ideas on the chessboard can repeat themselves in diverse positions. Each idea is itself the complex expression of a relationship between different pieces on the board. Correctly perceiving those relationships is an essential part of chess understanding and can come only with experience. Each time an essential pattern repeats itself in the experience of an individual player, that pattern is recognized more quickly. In time, each chess position is recognized not as a collection of disparate pieces on the board, but as a coherent series of interrelationships between those pieces. Each move made on the board will change some of those relationships, while leaving others unaltered. The whole position, and the flow of the game, can be seen as a mutating organism, making a sequence of discrete changes of form as each piece is moved.

Most important, therefore, as the game progresses, is to focus attention firstly on the last move played. As soon as the opponent has moved, one should look at that move and ask how it alters one's perception of the game. What new squares are threatened by the moving piece? What lines are possibly opened by the square it vacated? Was the piece performing any important function before it moved, which is now left unattended? And, of course, one should ask exactly the same questions of one's own intended moves before committing them to the board.

Acquiring such a discipline in thought processes is the only way to avoid those grievous mistakes which chess players know as blunders. The same discipline helps develop a pattern of thought which can cope with the organization of the widely diverse tactical elements which make up a single position.

1 It is part of essential tactical technique to train oneself to calculate all forcing variations from any position – and there is nothing more forcing than a move that delivers check. Here, for example, White might consider 1 Bf7+ which leads to mate after 2 ... Rxf7 3 Qxh7, or 2 ... Kh8 3 Qxh7.

Unfortunately, however, Black has a better reply. When you have found it, try looking at other forcing moves for White in the diagram position. One of them forces mate in two moves.

2 Here is a far more complex position: White to move in the game Rosentalis–Nikolic, Moscow 1994. The first thing to look at should be 1 Qh7+ Kf8 2 Qh8+ Ke7 (Black's reply is forced on each occasion). Now 3 Rxf7+ would be mate, if the Bishop could not take it, and that should be enough to see 3 Rxf7+ Bxf7 4 Rxf7 mate. The question is, though, what happens after 3 Rxf7+ Kd8? Can you find how White forces mate in a similar, but more brilliant fashion?

Hint: think about the essentials of the mating position after 4 Rxf7 above. The Queen uses only her rook's move to guard the back rank, while a Rook, protected on f7, gives check and the Pawn on e5 prevents an escape to d6. But how does White rid himself of the nuisance of the Bishop on e8?

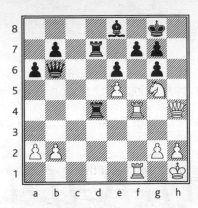

3 Finally, an example of a combination that does not end in checkmate. In this position, from a Petrosian–Spassky world championship game in 1966, White can play 1 N×f7, leaving himself a Pawn up after either K×f7 or Q×e3, but just think how strong N×f7 would be if it delivered check. The essence of any combination is to force the opponent's pieces into a desired geometrical configuration. What is the configuration here, and how does White make it come about?

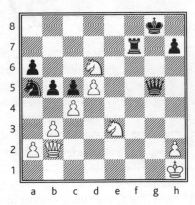

See Chapter 5 for answers.

4

principles of opening play

In this chapter we will consider the start of the game. The task during the opening of the game should be to ensure that your pieces are actively positioned and ready to cooperate with one another. Don't waste time letting your pieces be chased around the board and make sure you find a safe place for your King before the centre of the board becomes a dangerous place. This chapter will consider the three objectives that should be paramount in one's thoughts during the opening phase of the game: development of the pieces; control of the centre of the board; and the conquest of space. We will also look at the basic principles of sound and effective development and when it is appropriate to break the rules.

Development of the pieces

This means at its simplest bringing the men off the back rank, somewhere into the middle of the board where they might be of more use in threatening the enemy. At the very start of the game, however, one has no idea where the opponent is going to be putting his pieces, and consequently no idea where one's own men will be needed as the game progresses. As the pieces and Pawns are brought into play, the shape of the battle begins to take form. Each move made divulges more of a player's plans, and provides information about where both sides' men will be most effectively placed. Whichever side secures his own King's safety and mobilizes his other men more quickly will be the first to be in a position to launch an attack, so time is of the essence in the opening.

The principles of development to be remembered are as follows:

* bring all the pieces into play as quickly as possible
* castle early, to bring the Rooks into the game and the King into safety
* try to combine developing moves with attack on the opponent's undefended points
* do not lose time by allowing your pieces to be chased about as your opponent brings out his own men.

Remember too that Bishops need diagonals and Rooks need open files if they are to function effectively. Lines tend to be opened as Pawns advance and are exchanged, so one often has to wait before knowing where the Rooks are going to be most effective. Castling connects the two Rooks and eases their passage towards any file which may become open later in the game. Usually the decisions for Bishops are easier, since any Pawn advance is liable to open diagonals and point the way towards an effective Bishop deployment.

Control of the centre

The 'centre' is defined as the squares e4, d4, e5 and d5, and much of a well-played opening is centred around the struggle for control of those squares. The reason for this is simply understood: the centre is the hub of the chessboard, where attack and defence can meet, and where the King's side of the board rubs shoulders with the Queen's side. If one is to keep lines of communication open, control of the centre is essential. As the pattern of the game develops, it may easily become necessary to shift emphasis from attack to defence, or from one part of the board to another. Centrally placed pieces can move into action on all four corners of the board at a moment's notice, so until priorities become clear, the centre of the board remains the most useful and important area.

Just as one should give the greatest attention to the four squares which form the centre, the 12 squares surrounding them should also be treated with respect. The area bounded by c-file and f-file and by third and sixth ranks has been termed the 'little centre'. With more influence than the edge, and less than the full centre, those squares also form useful bases for pieces where they can maintain some flexibility of action.

Notice that throughout this brief explanation we have only referred to *control* of the centre, rather than occupation. It is more important to secure control of the central squares for use by one's pieces when they need them as transit stops between one half of the board and the other, than actually to occupy those squares too quickly. Occupation may often be a considerable aid towards ultimate gain of control, but as we shall see later, control may also be effected at a distance.

In early computer chess programs, opening strategy was simulated by attaching different values to different squares on the board. By scoring, say, three points each time a piece attacks one of the four centre squares, two points for an attack on any of the twelve little-centre squares, and one point for any other square on the board, the programmer simulates a view of the chessboard in which the edges are less important than the middle. The difficulty for the machine is to recognize when the centre of gravity of play moves from the geometrical centre of the board. A human player knows instinctively to move his pieces towards the sound of gunfire.

The centre may only be a useful stopping-off point on that journey of redeployment.

Until the early manoeuvres are completed, however, the centre is the most important place on the board. The player who controls the centre is well placed to dictate the future course of events and switch play at will from one side to the other.

The conquest of space

The *tactics* of chess are concerned mainly with the gain of material; the *strategy* may be associated with the gain of territory. Knights, Bishops, Queens and Rooks need safe squares from which to operate; equally important is the task of denying the opponent such safe squares for his own pieces. The chessman ideally suited to the job of the conquest of territory is the Pawn, for no piece of larger value dare tread where a Pawn may capture it. While bringing out one's men from the back rank, therefore, the Pawns may also be advanced, preparing safe ground for their later plans.

Achieving the correct balance between Pawn moves and moves of the other pieces in the opening is one of the more difficult problems of early development. Too many Pawn moves, and the opponent will gain time attacking those Pawns; too many piece moves and there is danger of those pieces being chased back by space-gaining Pawn advances of the opponent. The ideal balance is to make just enough Pawn moves to secure squares on which all the pieces can operate without fear of molestation. As we shall see in many examples, the Pawn moves are perhaps the most difficult in chess. Remember that the Pawns cannot move backwards: once a Pawn has renounced its control over a square by advancing, that control can never be regained.

Now let us see how these ideas work out in the formulation of a plan for the opening and the decision of what moves to play. A good idea is to begin the game with a pre-planned scheme of where all one's men will be positioned. That scheme may have to be modified with each move the opponent makes, and the final positions of all the pieces may bear only scant resemblance to the original design, but such a scheme gives something to work towards and helps towards deciding on the individual moves. The diagram below gives a sensible pattern of development to aim for. This diagram, and the two following, show only White pieces, as they represent a development scheme in White's mind, to be modified according to Black's play. Note the following important features:

* each piece has moved only once, avoiding loss of time
* all the men are centrally placed, prepared for any eventuality
* the Pawns at d4 and e4 occupy two centre squares and attack the other two at d5 and e5
* the White Rooks are connected and free to occupy a central file when one becomes open after exchanges of Pawns
* finally, the White King is safely castled behind a wall of defensive Pawns and ready to meet any attack.

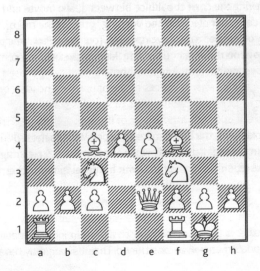

Now let us look at a sequence of opening moves and see how circumstances cause a modification of White's plans.

1 e4 e5

Already a change of plan is indicated. The Black Pawn covers both d4 and f4, squares which White wanted to utilize. Perhaps it was too much to hope that Black would allow our expansive formation so readily. A little contraction is called for: move the Bishop back from f4 to e3, the Pawn back from d4 to d3 to modify our ideal set-up.

2 Nf3 Nc6

Two functional developing moves; White brings his Knight into the game attacking a Pawn, Black's Knight rushes out to defend it.

3 Bc4 Bc5

Both Bishops are now well-placed on active, open diagonals. It is interesting to observe that the move 1 ... e5 by Black actually contributed to a weakening of the diagonal from a2 to f7. If that Pawn were still on e7, Black could move it to e6, placing a huge obstacle in the path of the White Bishop. Equally, White's 1 e4 could be considered to have lessened White's potential control of the diagonal from f2 to a7. Of course, one would not criticize either Pawn move on those accounts. Any Pawn move will lose control in some direction but gain it in another.

4 0-0 Nf6
5 d3 d6

Black's move attacked the e-Pawn, so White selected a move from his modified plan which defended it; equally 5 Nc3 might have been chosen. Either would fit in with his development scheme.

6 Nc3 0-0
7 Be3

Another move from the plan, but White might also have considered 7 Bg5, a move into the opponent's half of the board, invited by Black's chosen piece formation. Pinning the Knight to Black's Queen, White would restrict his opponent's freedom of action.

7 ... Bxe3
8 fxe3

We could say here that the opening is satisfactorily concluded. White has brought out his pieces and one more Queen move will leave his Rooks ready for action. The exchange of Bishops has created an open line for the Rook on f1 (the Knight can easily be moved from f3 to allow the Rook full scope) and White can begin to make plans for the middlegame.

The above moves are only given as an example of the formulation, modification and fulfilment of a plan of development for the opening.

Rules and when to break them

Beginners are besieged in chess books such as this with pieces of advice masquerading under the guise of chess principles, yet when they see games of Grandmasters, those principles seem to be broken all the time. Let us then look at some of these 'principles' and discover some of the real ideas which underlie them.

Rule 1: Do not bring your Queen out early

The logic of this rule is that the Queen, while a powerful attacking piece, is generally poor at fighting for control of the board. If the Queen is brought into play quickly, she becomes vulnerable to attack by the lighter pieces. Each time she is attacked, time is lost as she moves again.

On the other hand, it must be admitted that a centrally placed Queen does attack a large number of squares. If a central square does become available for the Queen, where she will be free from possibility of attack by enemy men, then she can exert a strong influence.

To illustrate this point, we might consider two similar opening sequences:

(a) *1* e4 e5 *2* d4 exd4 *3* Qxd4
(b) *1* e4 e5 *2* Nf3 Nc6 *3* d4 exd4 *4* Nxd4 Nxd4 *5* Qxd4

In the first case, we may criticize White for bringing his Queen out too early. By continuing 3 ... Nc6, Black brings a piece into the game, on an active square, and forces White to lose time moving his Queen away from attack.

In the second example, White's play is far less open to criticism. The only move which attacks the White Queen safely is 5 ... c5, a non-developing move which has the added defect of losing permanent control of the d5 square. After 6 Qe3, White can look forward to completing his development with Bc4, Nc3 and later establishing a piece in Black's half of the board on d5.

Returning to the position after 5 Qxd4, Black has another way of threatening the Queen: 5 ... Ne7 followed by Nc6, but that takes two moves and so in effect loses as much time for Black as for White.

In general it is a mistake to bring out Queens and Rooks when they will be able to be attacked by lighter pieces moving to effective squares. In doing so, your opponent will be proceeding towards a complete mobilization of his pieces, while your own development will lag behind as the Queen or Rook goes roaming alone.

Before leaving this theme, it is appropriate to quote opening moves of a truly terrible game lost by a primitive chess-playing computer program with the white pieces. The machine clearly appreciated the value of the centre squares which it desperately tried to control with its Queen. As an example of why such a strategy is flawed, these moves can hardly be improved upon:

1 e4 e5 *2* d4 exd4 *3* Qxd4 Nc6 *4* Qd5 Nf6 *5* Qf5 d5 *6* Qf4 Bd6 *7* Qg5 h6 *8* Qxg7 Rh7. White loses his Queen for the Rook, and still he has no pieces in play. Of course, loss of the Queen was not necessary, but by the time she fell, Black had gained total control of the central squares for which the Queen had been so vainly fighting.

Later in this chapter, we shall examine some less trivial examples of attempts to use the Queen early in the game in an attacking manner.

Rule 2: Do not move a piece more than once in the opening

In principle this ought to be good advice. If one can develop all one's men, moving each once only, then one will be ready for action more quickly than an opponent who potters about with each man, changing his mind about where it should stand. But let us look at a couple of sequences of opening moves:

(a) 1 e4 e5   2 Nf3 Nc6   3 Bb5 a6   4 Ba4 Nf6   5 0-0 b5   6 Bb3;

(b) 1 e4 Nf6   2 e5 Nd5   3 c4 Nb6   4 d4 d6.

The first of these examples sees the White Bishop moving three times within the first six moves, yet it is one of the most popular ways of beginning a game. The second sequence is also not uncommon, but Black's Knight has made three moves before anything else joins in the game at all. The key to understanding such play lies in looking at what the opponent is doing in each case. In neither example does the other player bring out any pieces while the moves are 'being wasted' by moving the same man. Both are examples of using repeated moves of one piece to lure forward the enemy Pawns, in the hope that those Pawns will be vulnerable later, or that their advances will leave areas of weakness behind them. Such a strategy is quite sophisticated (especially in example *b*, where Black actually invites the White Pawns to dominate the centre), but not as illogical as it may seem.

Rule 3: Knights before Bishops

In bygone days this was an oft-quoted rule of development, based on the idea that Knights could usually be relied upon to develop on f3, c3, f6 and c6, whereas it was usually advisable to wait until later before deciding where the Bishops would be at their most effective. There is, however, no inherent logic to the rule, except in positions where one is indeed confident that the

Knight will be well placed on those squares. In many modern opening systems, the role of the Bishop is decided first, then everything is done to ensure that its diagonal is kept free and uncluttered. What is good advice, however, is to play those moves essential to one's development plan before adding the optional extras.

Flexibility is the key to successful development, so options should be left open where possible.

In short, then, the only rule which really does pertain to opening play is the one which advises getting one's pieces into active play as quickly as possible. Delay is only permitted either to take advantage of an error by the opponent or to induce a comparable delay in the opponent's development plans.

We have already examined one sequence of opening moves in which White began with an ideal position for his pieces, then had to modify that ideal as Black's moves appeared on the board. Of course, there are very many possible development schemes which one may adopt as ideal. Before ending this brief discussion of the opening, let us look at two more of the vast number of acceptable schemes of development, just to give an idea of what one should be thinking about when bringing out the pieces.

Remember always that the scheme of development should be determined within the first few moves. It will undergo constant modification, but the plans will only be scrapped if tactical circumstances of such overwhelming importance arise that instant action is demanded.

The following two positions illustrate widely differing patterns of pieces, but both fully conform with our principles: the pieces are brought into play, Kings castled into safety, and the centre of the board is kept under close surveillance. Such a pattern of pieces is described as an *opening system* and the most important systems have names attached to them, usually the names of their originators or of the great players who first gave popularity to the system.

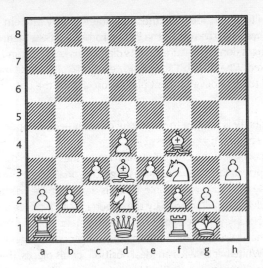

In the development plan illustrated above, White has been realistically modest in his aims. He has a firm foothold in the centre, with the d-Pawn strongly supported. White's pieces put in a good claim for control of e4 and e5, both Bishops have good diagonals and the Queen is ready to play to c2 or e2 putting her weight behind the white-squared Bishop. The h3 Pawn move is an interesting accessory: in the long term, it may serve to provide the King an escape square on h2 in case of a back-rank mate threat, but more immediately it provides a retreat for the Bishop on f4. By playing e3 after Bf4, White has cut off its retreat in one direction. Normally one would be reluctant to play such a move as h3, just in case the Bishop needed a retreat, but such a move can often turn out to be an indispensable part of an opening scheme. Note also how White has tended to develop his pieces behind his central Pawns, leaving those Pawns free to advance and gain space later in the game. The order of White's moves might easily have been d4, Nf3, Bf4, e3, Bd3, 0-0, Nbd2, h3, c3. Alternatively, White could have opted for a more aggressive plan with c4 and Nc3 in place of the restrained c3 and Nbd2; again the Knight develops behind the Pawn to facilitate its later advance.

The next position illustrates a completely different, but equally valid approach to the problem of development in the opening.

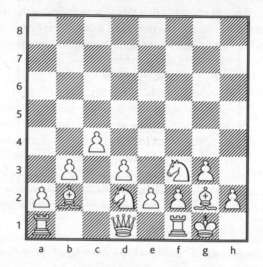

Here the essential feature is the development of the Bishops. Placing them at b2 and g2, they are on their longest diagonals and their influence has not been interrupted by putting Pawns at d4 or e4. The Knight on f3 lessens the immediate power of the g2-Bishop, but its strength may be felt since the Knight is fully able to move away and uncover the Bishop whenever it chooses. White's Pawns on d3 and c4, controlling e4 and d5 respectively, enhance the prospects of the white-squared Bishop. The Knight on f3 and Bishop on b2 both add their weight to control of d4 and e5. So although White has been more reticent in advancing his centre Pawns, the theme of his development structure is still very much one of central control.

The structure on the White's King's side is very commonly seen in modern chess. It is known as a *fianchetto* development of the Bishop (from the Italian, meaning 'little flank'). By extension, any development of a Bishop to g2 or b2 (g7 or b7 in Black's case) is called a fianchetto of the Bishop.

The attack on f7

We have already met two drastically short games: scholar's mate and fool's mate. In the first, White attacked f7 with Bishop and Queen; Black missed the point and allowed Qxf7 mate on move four. In fool's mate, White lost in two moves by advancing f-Pawn and g-Pawn to allow Qh4 mate. These quick games share a common theme – the weakness of the f-Pawn.

The square on which the f-Pawn starts the game, and the diagonal connecting the Pawn with its King, are the most vulnerable areas in early play. Many games are won by single-minded attacks on f7 or f2, but they ought not to be. With so many pieces clustered round the King, it takes a degree of carelessness for the defender to fall foul of such quick attacks. Let us look more closely at some possible continuations if White's immediate attack is met by sensible defence. We shall begin with the opening moves of scholar's mate:

1 e4 e5 2 Bc4 Bc5 3 Qh5

White attacks e5 and f7, so Black must find a move to protect both those Pawns:

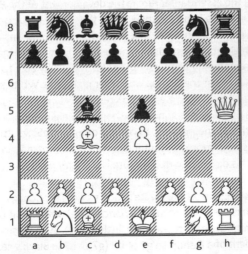

3 ... Qe7

Equally, Black might choose *3 ... Qf6* attacking f2 himself. After *3 ... Qe7*, Black can look forward to gaining time with Nf6, attacking the White Queen. After, for example, *4 Nc3* (hoping to attack the Black Queen with Nd5) *4 ... Nf6 5 Qg5 0-0* Black's development is well advanced. *6 Nd5?* would even lose a piece to *6 ... Nxd5* (discovering an attack on the Queen) *7 Qxe7 Nxe7*.

Instead of *4 Nc3*, it is more interesting to examine the consequences of **4 Nf3**. White attacks e5 and even prepares another attack on f7 with Ng5. We might consider a number of continuations:

(a) *4 ... Nf6 5 Qxe5 Nxe4 6 Qxe7+ Bxe7* and White's 'attack' has led only to an exchange of Queens;

(b) *4 ... Nc6 5 Ng5 Nd8 6 Nxh7?* (Better *6 0-0* or *6 Nc3*) *g6!* *7 Qh3 d5!* attacking Bishop and Queen and winning a piece at least. Note in this sequence how *6 ... g6* defended against the threat of Nf6+ by opening the line between f6 and h8 and ensuring that Qxf6 would defend the Black Rook.

(c) *4 ... d6 5 Ng5 Nh6 6 Nc3 c6* (keeping the Knight out of d5) *7 0-0 Nd7 8 d3 Nf6 9 Qh4 d5 10 exd5 Nf5!* *11 Qh3* (the only safe square) *11 ... Ne3!* (discovering an attack on the Queen) *12 Qf3* (*12 Qh4* is better, when Black has the choice from *12 ... Nxf1*, *12 ... Nxd5* or repeating position with *12 ... Nf5*) *12 ... Bg4 13 Qg3 Nf5* and the White Queen has nowhere to run. Of course, that was a rather drastic example of punishment for early Queen development, but typical of the sort of mess liable to happen when an optimistic Queen sortie is followed by further inaccuracy.

The characteristic defences to f7 were all illustrated in those variations: Qe7 or Qf6, Nh6, and 0-0 are the most usual ways to protect f7, with Nd8 (retreating from c6) a less common resource from the defensive armoury. Now let us examine a more subtle way to attack the f-Pawn, not with Queen and Bishop, but with Bishop and Knight. The following opening moves are very common:

1 e4 e5
2 Nf3 Nc6
3 Bc4

The Bishop is already bearing down on the vulnerable Pawn and the Knight stands ready to add his weight from g5 if Black allows it. (That square, of course, is defended by the Queen at the moment.)

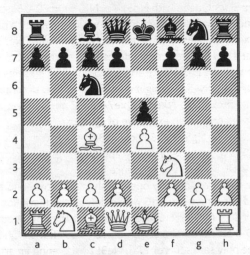

Now Black has a number of perfectly adequate moves: 3 ... Be7, 3 ... Bc5 or 3 ... d6 all conform to opening principles (though the last of these lets out one Bishop at the expense of blocking a path for the other). The natural developing move

3 ... Nf6

is a little incautious, however, since it has the effect of blocking the Queen's view of g5. White can now play

4 Ng5

and Black has none of his normally available defences to f7: he cannot yet castle, and his Queen is too heavy a defender – after 4 ... Qe7 5 Bxf7+, Black would come off far worse from the exchanges on f7. The only move to counter the attack on f7 is to block the Bishop's diagonal with

4 ... d5.

Let us see how that came to grief in an 1858 game won by Paul Morphy:

5 exd5 Nxd5

Surprisingly, a mistake; Black should attack the Bishop with 5 ... Na5 and later chase the Knight with h6. He may never regain his Pawn, but he drives back the attackers and gains much time. In this manner 3 ... Nf6 becomes a playable move after all.

6 d4!

White plays to mobilize his forces as quickly as possible. Instead 6 Qf3 Qxg5 7 Bxd5 Nd8 or in this line 7 Qxd5 Be6 would have got White nowhere. The tempting continuation was 6 Nxf7 Kxf7 7 Qf3+, forcing the Black King to e6 if he wants to save the Knight on d5. Morphy's idea is based on the same theme.

6 ... exd4
7 0-0 Be7 (see diagram)

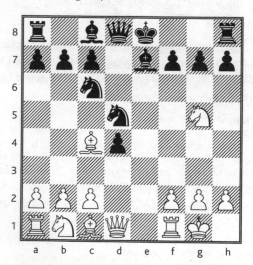

Given one more move, Black would castle out of danger. White's whole theme has been to attack the King in the centre. His next move invests a Knight to keep the monarch under fire.

8 Nxf7! Kxf7
9 Qf3+ Ke6

Otherwise White will simply regain his piece with *10 Bxd5*

10 Nc3!

This new investment is to open more lines of attack and allow the a1-Rook to join in without delay.

10 ... dxc3
11 Re1+ Ne5
12 Bf4 Bf6

White utilizes the power of his pins very instructively. Now follows a demolition job to complete the exposure of the Black King:

13 Bxe5 Bxe5
14 Rxe5+! Kxe5
15 Re1+ Kd4

15 ... Kd6 16 Qxd5 would already be checkmate.

16 Bxd5 Re8

16 ... Qxd5 would have allowed *17 Qxc3* mate, but Black's King has been forced too far away from home for the defenders to come to his aid against the attacking force of Queen, Rook and Bishop.

17 Qd3+ Kc5
18 b4+ Kxb4
19 Qd4+

And Black is mated whichever way he runs: *19 ... Ka5 20 Qxc3+ Ka6 21 Qa3+ Kb5 (or b6) 22 Rb1 mate*; or *19 ... Ka5 20 Qxc3+ Ka4 21 Qb3+ Ka5 22 Qa3+ Kb6 (or b5) 23 Rb1 mate*; or *19 ... Kb5 20 Rb1+ Ka5 21 Qb4+ Ka6 22 Qb5 mate*; or *19 ... Ka3 20 Qxc3+ Ka4 21 Qb3+ as before.* With nowhere to hide the Black King is quickly gunned down in the wide open spaces. You should be able to work out some other mates for yourself.

That game should be enough to demonstrate the importance of castling early in the game as well as showing how a lead in development can be exploited dramatically if the position is sufficiently open.

5

chess in the computer age

Advances in technology in the closing years of the twentieth century had a massive impact on the game of chess. In the space of a few decades, computer chess advanced from mindless ineptitude to Grandmaster, or even world championship, strength while the Internet enabled the instant spread of chess information and brought competitive chess to a wider number of people than ever before.

Yet over the past couple of decades, the growing power of computers has dealt a heavy blow to human vanity. Not so long ago, we used to laugh at the feeble attempt of machines to play chess; now we can only look in awe at the quality of play produced by their phenomenal calculating speed. The strengths and remaining weakness of computer chess will both be seen in this chapter.

Computer chess

Until the 1980s, the world's strongest chess players were generally scornful of attempts to program computers to beat them at chess. Machines were very good at avoiding blunders or working out sequences of checks or captures, but when it came to matters of fine positional judgement, they were floundering. The number-crunching silicon brains simply did not understand the subtleties of the game. Good chess, like art, or musical composition, or novel writing, had more to it than mere calculation.

We even devised positions to demonstrate the limitations of computer thought. Take the diagram below, for example. It is White to play; what would you do?

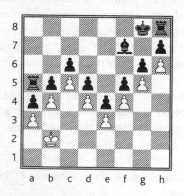

The enlightened human player sees quickly that the position is irrevocably blocked. If White just shuffles his King to and fro, there is nothing Black can ever do. The Black Rooks and Bishop are trapped behind the chain of Pawns and can never do any damage. The only thing White has to avoid doing is making any captures. After, for example, 1 bxa5, Black will play Be6, followed by Kf7; his remaining Rook will round up the white a-Pawn, and eventually Black will advance his Pawn, freed by White's injudicious capture, to b4, unblocking the position and forcing a way through for his pieces.

The typical computer, however, naively thinks it's better to be one Rook and a Bishop down than two Rooks and a Bishop down, so it takes the black Rook.

Positions such as these seemed to confirm that some aspects of chess would always be beyond mechanical calculation. If there was a forced checkmate in two or three, or perhaps even ten or twelve moves, a computer would find it, by sheer brute force of calculation, within seconds, but subtle strategic aspects would remain beyond its silicon horizons. Or so we smugly believed.

Around 1990, however, all that began to change. Even 20 years earlier, a tendency had been noticed that should have been worrying for human supremacists: a strong relationship had been noticed between increases in a computer's processing speed and its chess rating. Programming techniques were constantly being improved and refined, it is true, but nothing had as much effect as the sheer speed of calculation, allowing more and more possibilities to be analysed more and more deeply. Studies have suggested that the average human player looks at around 500 positions before selecting his next move. Computers looking at 500,000 positions could not play so well because we were so much better at deciding which positions were worth looking at. When machines started thinking at a rate of around one million positions a second, however, a qualitative leap in their performance became apparent.

A human might, without any real calculation at all, reject a certain Pawn move because it weakened a particular square where an enemy piece might, at some unspecified time in the future, land with powerful effect. Now computers were rejecting such weakening moves, and one had a strong feeling that they had seen as far as the moment when an enemy piece did land on the square. To make life even more difficult, sometimes they did play moves that humans would reject instinctively, knowing that they could get away with them.

When Garry Kasparov, then World Champion, was beaten by the IBM computer Deep Blue in 1998, the machine was analysing at an incredible rate of 100 million positions a second. Even the best player can wilt under that sort of pressure.

Deep Blue–Kasparov, Philadelphia 1996
Sicilian Defence

In 1996, the world's strongest chess player faced the world's most powerful chess computer in a challenge match. 'Deep Blue' was a project that had begun in the 1970s as a chess program called Deep Thought, which became the first to win a tournament ahead of human Grandmasters. In 1990, its programmers were recruited by IBM for a mission with the stated aim of defeating the World Champion.

Making a billion calculations and looking at up to a hundred million chess positions every second, Deep Blue was clearly a formidable opponent. Kasparov had lost to computers before, but only in quick-play games where fast time limits created greater hazards for human fallibility. This match, however, was at the normal tournament rate, which allocated each player two hours for 40 moves. When Kasparov was beaten in the opening game, it was the first time a machine had beaten the World Champion under such conditions.

The game proceeded as follows:

1 e4 c5 2 c3 d5 3 exd5 Qxd5 4 d4 Nf6 5 Nf3 Bg4 6 Be2 e6 7 h3 Bh5 8 0-0 Nc6 9 Be3 cxd4 10 cxd4 Bb4 11 a3 Ba5 12 Nc3 Qd6

The position is one of a type of dynamic equilibrium common in top-class chess. The Pawn on d4 controls c5 and e5, either of which could be an important outpost in a future White attack. By comparison, the Black Pawn on e6 has a primarily defensive function. The Pawn on d4, however, is isolated and may become vulnerable later in the game.

13 Nb5

A very machine-like move. Most strong human players would not be tempted by this attack on the Queen. White may gain a move now by forcing the Queen to move, but the Knight will almost certainly be forced back in a move or two when Black plays ... a6 and the whole manoeuvre will end up losing time. On this occasion, however, the machine proves to be correct.

13 ... Qe7 14 Ne5 Bxe2 15 Qxe2 0-0 16 Rac1 Rac8 17 Bg5! Bb6 18 Bxf6 gxf6

Recapturing with the Queen would have allowed a Knight fork on d7.

19 Nc4 Rfd8

And here, *19 ... Bxd4 20 Nxd4 Nxd4* runs into a Queen fork with *21 Qg4+*.

20 Nxb6 axb6 21 Rfd1 f5 22 Qe3 Qf6 23 d5! Rxd5 24 Rxd5 exd5 25 b3!

Calmly safeguarding its b-Pawn, Deep Blue knows that it will regain the Pawn on b6, leaving Black with many weak Pawns. Note that *25 ... d4* is simply met by *26 Nxd4*, exploiting the pin along the c-file.

25 ... Kh8 26 Qxb6 Rg8 27 Qc5 d4 28 Nd6 f4 29 Nxb7 Ne5 30 Qd5 f3 31 g3 Nd3 32 Rc7 Re8 33 Nd6 Re1+ 34 Kh2 Nxf2

Given one more move, Black could deliver checkmate with Rh1. Sadly, he never gets the chance.

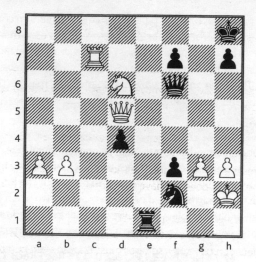

35 Nxf7+ Kg7

Black could try *35 Qxf7*, hoping for *36 Qxf7? Rh1* mate, but White plays instead *37 Qd8+!* winning easily after either *37 ... Re8 38 Qxd4+* or *37 ... 38 Qf6+*.

36 Ng5+ Kh6 37 Rxh7+ Black resigned.

After *37 ... Kg6* there follows *38 Qg8+ Kf5 39 Nxf3*, stopping Black's mate threat and leaving White three Pawns up with a winning attack.

Despite this defeat, Kasparov went on to win the match by three victories to one with two draws, but in 1998, an improved, and even faster version of Deep Blue defeated Kasparov in a new match, with three wins, one loss and two draws from their six games. Having achieved their ambition, IBM declined Kasparov's challenge to a return match saying that Deep Blue had better things to do with its time than play chess.

Answers to exercises

Chapter 1

1a A Knight takes three moves to make such a one-square trip. For example, to reach b1 from a1, it may move a1–b3–d2–b1, or a1–c2–a3–b1.

1b Only two moves, in general; for example, from c3 to d4, it may travel via b5 or via e2. The only exception is when one of the two squares is a corner square. The trip from a1 to b2 takes four moves (the Knight does not have the turning space to do it in two moves).

1c Six moves; for example a1–b3–d4–e6–f4–g6–h8. Note that the Knight changes the colour of the square it occupies each move, so a trip between two black squares must take an even number of moves.

2 Either side could deliver checkmate. If it is White's move, then *1* f7 is mate. The Pawn threatens the King, which cannot move to any square not under fire from the White Bishop or Pawn. Neither can the Pawn be captured by Black's King, since it is defended by the other White Pawn.

If it is Black's move, any move by the Rook will put the White King in check from the Bishop (such a check by a non-moving piece is termed a 'discovered check'). The one such move which denies the White King any escape square is *1* ... Rg5, preventing *2* Kg1 because of the check from the Rook.

3 After *1* ... b5+, White's King has no move to escape from the check, but it is not checkmate. The only move is to capture the Pawn en passant. So White plays *2* cxb6 e.p. (en passant captures are generally recorded in this manner – the White c-Pawn makes a capture on b6, note, not on b5). If we look at the resulting position, we see that Black is in stalemate. None of his men can move without exposing his King to check, but he is not in check at the moment. The game is a draw.

Chapter 3

1 After *1 Bf7+ Kxf7* White has no good way to continue the attack. Instead *1 Qxh7+!* forces *1 ... Kxh7* when *2 Bf7!* is discovered check and mate. Note how the Bishop uses its move to control the g8 square.

2 White forces mate with *4 Qxe8+! Kxe8 5 Rf8+ Ke7 6 R1f7* mate. The final position is another, rather elaborate variation on the standard two-Rooks mate.

3 White played *1 Qh8+!!* forcing *1 ... Kxh8* when *2 Nxf7+* forked King and Queen. After *2 ... Kg7* or *2 ... Kg8*, White plays *3 Nxg5* remaining a Knight and a Pawn ahead.